Ants and Ants

By Liza Charlesworth

ISBN: 978-1-339-02672-5

Art Director: Tannaz Fassihi; Designer: Tanya Chernyak
Photos © Getty Images.
Copyright © Liza Charlesworth. All rights reserved. Published by Scholastic Inc.

3 4 5 6 7 8 9 10   68   32 31 30 29 28 27 26 25 24

Printed in Jiaxing, China. First printing, August 2023.

■SCHOLASTIC

See the ant stand
on top of the ants.
Ants can help ants!

See the ant on the hand.
It has six legs.
It is not a big bug.

See the ants on the plants.
Ants can be red and
ants can be black.

Ants make hills in the grass.
Ants make hills on the sand.

An ant can pick up a lot!
It can pick up bits of a plant.
Lug, lug, lug!

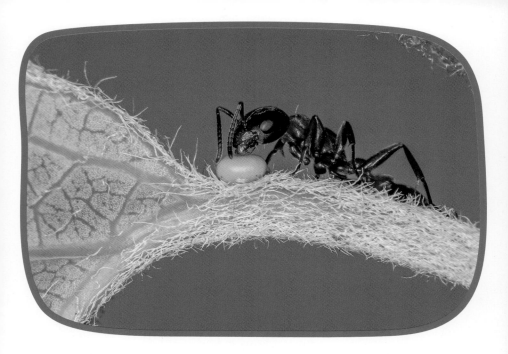

An ant can snack on plants.
It can snack on sap, pods,
and eggs as well.

An ant is not big.
But an ant is grand!